EASY TO MAKE

SCENTED GIFTS

$\mathscr{E}$ASY TO MAKE
SCENTED GIFTS
JUDY TAYLOR

ANAYA PUBLISHERS LTD LONDON

First published in Great Britain in 1994
by Anaya Publishers Ltd, Strode House,
44–50 Osnaburgh Street, London NW1 3ND

Editor Val Jackson
Design Watermark Communications Ltd
Photographer Shona Wood
Artwork and illustrations Kate Simunek

British Library Cataloguing in Publication Data

Taylor, Judy
Easy to Make Scented Gifts. – (Easy to
Make Series)
I. Title II. Series
745.5

ISBN 1-85470-167-3

Typeset by Servis Filmsetting Ltd, Manchester, UK
Colour reproduction by Scantrans Pte Ltd, Singapore
Printed in Hong Kong

CONTENTS

Introduction

From ancient times, aromatic potions and oils have been added to gifts to make them more pleasing. Here this charming old custom is revived for modern times.

People have enjoyed using perfume in their everyday lives since the dawn of civilization.

In days when personal hygiene and sanitation were not as highly considered as they are now, fragrant oils and essences were a very important part of life for those who could afford them. Certainly they were used by the Greeks, Romans and Egyptians and it was quite a common custom for sweet-smelling rose petals and herbs to be strewn on to the paths of processions, when the air must have been heady with crushed, mingled fragrances. Perhaps this is where the modern tradition of scattering rose petals at wedding parties originated.

Cleopatra loved perfumes and must have spent her life drifting about on a cloud of it. To this day she is remembered for her exotic habit of bathing in scented oils.

No doubt her love of perfume did not go unnoticed by courtiers and servants wishing to gain favour.

More recent times

As recently as the fifteenth century, posies and pomanders filled with herbs were carried by noblemen and women to help mask foul odours, and layers of lavender and other herbs were placed between stored gowns and cloaks to prevent moth and to sweeten the garments. Every large house had its own herb garden for medicinal and cosmetic use and plants were gathered and made into soaps, creams and sometimes candles.

By the eighteenth century, manufactured perfumes were being sold all over Europe and though the old country fragrances were still made at home (Carmelite nuns used to make fragrant waters), they were not as necessary as they had been.

Fragrances for today

Nowadays, unwrapping a scented present gives the receiver added pleasure. It may be a beautifully-presented bowl of fragrant pot pourri, bringing into the

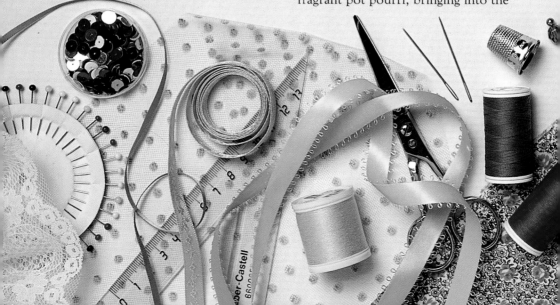

house all the lovely aromas of a spring garden or a dried flower arrangement with the spicey tang of a woodland walk redolent of the scent of moss, pine and citrus. A pillow containing the elusive reminder of rain-washed roses and sweet carnations cannot fail to please. There are many varied and unusual ways of making and giving scented gifts, most of them very simple.

Some perfumes you give may have been forgotten for years and their arrival will often evoke nostalgic memories.

Natural herbs, spices and flowers can be used to great effect; gifts can be designed for pretty and often practical purposes throughout the house. Linen bags and sachets, padded coat hangers, sleep pillows and cushions filled with hidden perfume will all give a delightful ambience to a room.

Try making herb garlands and mixtures of dried flowers and herbs which will keep insects at bay in the kitchen. Make a special statement for a birthday or wedding party with miniature arrangements of scented flowers or bridesmaids' gifts.

For a little girl, what could be prettier than a perfumed lavender lady doll or a dainty basket of tiny scented flowers?

Flower pomanders and lace sachets are romantic gifts for a wedding, as are scented shoe fillers, a lacey perfumed garter and a hidden satin heart for the 'something blue' which, tradition has it,

is supposed to be worn by brides. Bowls of pot pourri, perfumed notepaper, cards, wrapping paper and even scented inks are easy but effective gifts which will remind people of the care you took to create a special gift.

Essential oils

It will repay you to investigate the whole range of essential oils available.

A basket of pine cones with a few drops of essential oil added and placed by the fire, soon permeates the room with lovely woodland smells.

Some can be added to pot pourri recipes to give an invigorating and refreshing smell, while others have more relaxing, soporific qualities.

You will soon discover new ways of making and presenting scented gifts to create an atmosphere of romance or nostalgia, or merely as fun for your friends. These suggestions and ideas are bound to help you to make your gifts doubly welcome.

In the instructions, the specific materials you will need to make each item are listed, but not the basic materials needed for any craft work, such as scissors, needles and thread. If any unusual materials are required, they will be listed.

ONE

Hidden fragrance

Flower collage

A dainty dressing table gift made of small dried flowers, carefully stuck in a heart-shaped picture frame and brushed with essential rose oils to give lasting fragrance.

Materials
3 × 3in (7.5 × 7.5cm) heart-shaped picture
   frame
White card to fit inside frame
All-purpose adhesive
Dried deep pink rosebud
Dried blue larkspur flowers
Dried pink larkspur flowers
Dried white statice flowers
Dried pale green grasses
Rose oil

Preparation
1 Remove the backing from the picture frame and discard the front glass. Measure and cut the card to fit snugly inside the frame.

2 Draw a light pencil line all round the card to mark the edge of the frame.

3 Draw a cross on the heart from side to side and from top to bottom, to mark the centre of the card.

4 Sort out the dried material, choosing the smallest flowers and grasses. Trim off the stalks to make a flat surface for easier sticking.

5 Brush a thin layer of adhesive on to the card.

Vary the design
You can use different colours to vary the design. A dried daisy in the centre, for example, could be surrounded with gold and amber coloured flowers, then brushed with sandalwood oil.

Working the design
6 Trim off the stalk of the dried rosebud, add a dab of adhesive and press it firmly on to the middle of the card.

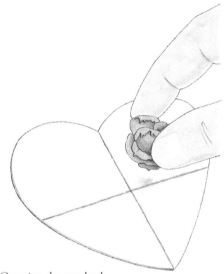

Centring the rosebud.

7 Choosing small flowers, press a circle of dried blue larkspur round the rosebud, making sure the flowers are attached firmly. Follow with a half circle of pink larkspur flowers.

8 On top of the heart, press on some white statice and a few grass seeds to complete the heart design. Do not place any flowers beyond the outline pencil mark. Allow to dry.

9 Very carefully, place the completed heart in the frame, making sure it is positioned centrally. Snap on the backing, then brush the rosebud with rose oil to give it lasting perfume.

Sachets

An easy-to-make bag can be made out of a lace handkerchief, filled with pot pourri. Here are some different sachets to sew which can be included in the gift projects.

Materials
(For one round sachet)
Two 4in (10cm)-diameter circles of fabric
24 × ½in (61cm × 13mm) wide lace
Pot pourri
12in (30.5cm) bead trim

To make the sachet
1 With right sides together and taking a ¼in (6mm) seam allowance, baste and machine-stitch round the outside of the circles, leaving a small opening for filling.

2 Turn right sides out. Baste a lace frill round the outside edge of the circles, including the opening.

3 Fill the sachet with pot pourri. Hand sew the opening to close it, then continue sewing the lace frill all the way round the circle. Remove the basting stitches.

4 Sew on bead trim.

Materials
(For one plain sachet)
8½ × 3in (21.5 × 7cm) fabric
Pot pourri

Preparation
1 With right sides facing, fold fabric in half to form a shape 4¼ × 5in (11 × 12.5cm). Taking a ¼in (6mm) seam allowance, machine-stitch along the two longer sides.

A heart-shaped sachet. Scale: 1sq = ½in (1.2cm)

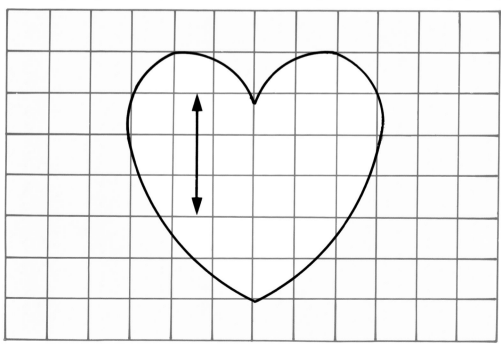

12

2 Turn right sides out and fill with pot pourri.

3 Sew the open end securely.

Materials
(For one heart-shaped sachet)
Two 4 × 4in (10 × 10cm) fabric pieces
4ins (10cm)-wide length of lace
$\frac{1}{8}$in (3mm)-wide length of satin ribbon
Pot pourri

Preparation
1 Draw the graph pattern on squared pattern paper. Cut out the pattern piece. Pin to the fabric and cut out two pieces.

Working the design
2 With right sides together and taking a $\frac{1}{4}$in (6mm) seam allowance, baste and machine-stitch the sides together. Leave a small opening at the top of the heart. Turn right sides out.

3 Baste a lace frill round the outside edge of the heart, including the top of the heart. Fill the heart with pot pourri.

4 Hand-sew the opening to close it, then continue sewing the lace frill all the way round the heart. Remove the basting stitches.

5 Make satin bows and sew them on to the front of the heart.

13

Decorated straw hat

This traditional-style straw hat will make a delightful gift – or an unusual wall hanging. Decorated with dried flowers, it has the added novelty of a hidden scent.

Materials
A medium-sized straw hat
36 × 5in (91.5 × 12cm) lace ribbon
12 × 2½in (30.5 × 6cm) satin ribbon
All purpose adhesive
Dried blue larkspur flowers
Dried golden rod flowers
Dried pale green grasses
Small sachet of pot pourri

Preparation
1 Cut off the flower heads and work out the design.

2 Attach the sachet of pot pourri to the inside of the straw hat, sticking it on firmly.

Working the design
3 Fold the lace ribbon in half widthways and stick the folded end to the back of the hat to form a double streamer. Cut the ends of the streamer diagonally. Make a bow of satin ribbon and stick that on top of the lace ribbon at the point where the crown meets the brim of the hat.

4 Spread adhesive in a small circle on top of the hat. Press larkspur flowers firmly on the adhesive circle, followed by a small circle of separate golden rod flowers. Stick a thick layer of larkspur flowers around the base of the crown, adding a double layer on the front brim of the hat.

5 Stick a small cluster of golden rod and larkspur flowers on either side of the brim. At the back of the hat on either side of the lace streamer, stick grasses, golden rod and larkspur in a fan shape.

6 Stick a small line of larkspur down the centre of the lace ribbon from the brim of the hat to about half way down the length of the lace ribbon.

By changing the flowers on the hat and also the pot pourri mixture, you can create a completely different mood. For a romantic design, use roses and lavender heads with pink grasses, decorated with pale pink ribbon.

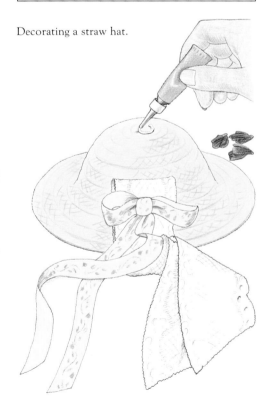

Decorating a straw hat.

Basket of small dried flowers

This pretty arrangement of tiny flowers is easy to make but very effective. Use a basket like this to decorate a bedroom or as a present for a small girl.

Materials
Small pink basket
Florist's dry foam
Small dried pink helichrysum
Dried statice
Small dried rosebuds
Dried sea lavender
Dried alchemilla
Several 5in (12.5cm)-long narrow pink
   ribbons in coordinated shades
Patchouli oil

Preparation
1 Take time to select only the very smallest flowers, snipping the tips off the sea lavender and taking only dainty pieces of statice.

2 Shape a piece of florist's dry foam and fit it firmly into the basket, making sure it does not slip about.

Working the design
3 Starting at the centre of the basket, push small pieces of helichrysum in to the foam.

4 Push small pieces of statice in to the foam round the edge of the basket.

5 Follow with the other flowers, forming an even dome shape. Work until the florist's foam is completely hidden.

6 Remember to push some flowers very close in to the foam and others less far in, as this will give more interest and movement to the arrangement.

7 Make a double bow of ribbons and attach it to the handle of the basket. Leave the ribbon ends hanging freely.

8 Perfume the flowers with a few drops of patchouli oil.

Basket of small
dried flowers

Many differently-shaped baskets can be found in florist's shops, each one presenting a challenge for the arranger, but if you are unable to find a basket easily, a prettily-shaped box or bowl will make an attractive substitute.

Shell with dried flowers

Capture the beauty of foam-capped waves with a shell from the sea shore, filled with dried flowers. Add some fragrant oil and use it as a bathroom decoration.

Materials
Sea shell
Florists' dry foam
Cotton wool
Lavender oil
Dried green grasses
Dried sea lavender
Dried pink delphinium
Dried deep pink corn heads

Preparation
1 It is important to choose flowers that are evocative of the sea and shore. Look for those that are varied in shape and have interesting colours and movement.

2 Shape a piece of florist's foam to fit in to the cavity of the shell.

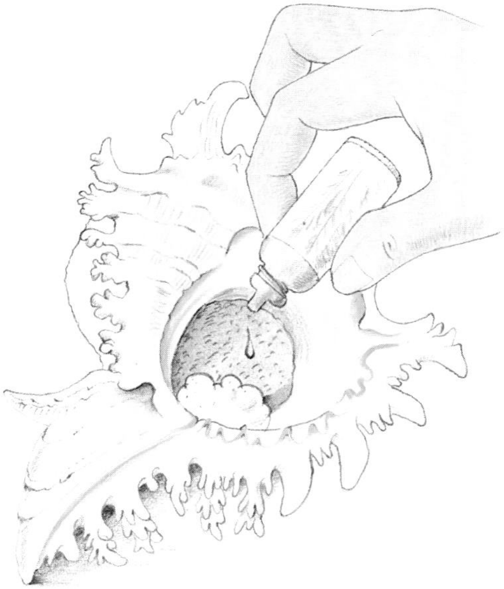

3 Make a small plug of cotton wool and press it firmly in to the shell cavity alongside the foam. Drop lavender oil on to the cotton wool.

4 Start the arrangement by pushing pieces of grass and sea lavender in to the foam, to make a pleasing outline.

5 Try to achieve a wave-shaped design by letting the flowers flow freely from the shell.

6 Arrange the rest of the flowers, remembering to place the larger ones close to the centre of the shell.

There are many differently-shaped sea shells to choose from. Some are spikey like the one shown here, others are quite smooth. Their colours will vary from soft pinks and browns to pale purples and white or cream. All purple, cream and blue flowers would go well with most shells.

A group of dried flowers arranged in shells would make an unusual table or sideboard decoration suitable for a festive occasion.
   A Christmas arrangement could be made using red flowers and green foliage with the addition of dried grasses sprayed with silver or gold paint.

Adding perfume to the inside of the shell.

18

Lavender lady

This little 'granny' doll is bound to be a great favourite with small girls. She is easily made out of scraps of fabric and is filled with lavender.

Materials
6in (15cm)-diameter circle of flesh-coloured stockinette for the head
Two 1in (2.5cm)-diameter circles of flesh-coloured stockinette for hands
Polyester wadding
Red thread
Black thread
11in (28cm) thick white cotton thread
$26 \times \frac{1}{8}$in (66cm × 3mm) ribbon
19×10in (48 × 25.5cm) piece of lavender-coloured fabric for body
$4\frac{1}{2}$in (11.5cm)-diameter circle of lavender-coloured fabric
Dried lavender
4in (10cm)-diameter circle of card
$35 \times 7\frac{1}{2}$in (89 × 19cm) piece of lavender-coloured fabric for skirt
$130 \times 1\frac{1}{2}$in (330 × 3.5cm) lace
30×1in (76 × 2.5cm) lace
$19 \times 6\frac{1}{2}$in (48 × 16.5cm) striped fabric for apron

Stitching the nose.

Preparation
1 Sew running stitches round the outside of the head and hand circles, stuff with polyester wadding and draw up the stitches to form three ball shapes.

2 Embroider two eyes in black and a mouth in red. Pencil in the eyebrows.

3 Sew a tiny circle of stitches in the middle of the face and draw it into a circle with a small amount of wadding inside, to form a nose.

4 Sew the strands of thick white cotton thread on the head with a line of stitches from the forehead to the nape of the neck, to make hair.

Sewing on the hair.

5 Stitch the hair to the head at the ear points and draw in to two bunches on either side of the face.

6 Plait the bunches and secure the ends of the plaits with ribbon.

Working the design
7 Using the body pattern, cut out one piece of fabric. Fold the body pattern at the fold line and stitch round the edges taking a ¼in (6mm) seam allowance and leaving the base open.

8 Fill the body with polyester wadding and a scattering of dried lavender.

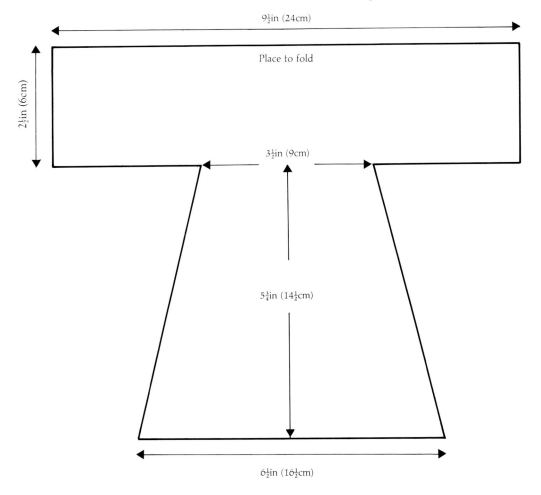

Pattern dimensions for the body of the doll.

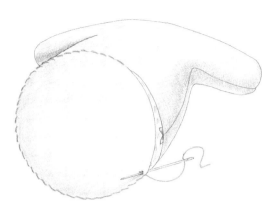

Sewing on the base of the doll.

9 Oversew the lavender-coloured fabric circle with the card circle inside, to the base of the doll, tucking in the raw edges.

10 Run a line of stitching round the ends of the arms and gather the stitching to form a wrist. Sew on the hands.

11 Sew the head to the centre of the arms.

12 Make the skirt by stitching the short ends of the rectangle together. Hem the bottom edge of the skirt. Gather up a length of 1½in (3.5cm) wide lace, baste it to the bottom hem, then stitch in place.

13 Gather the skirt top by sewing running stitches round the top edge of the skirt. Draw the stitches up and fit the skirt tightly round the doll to form a waist.

14 Make an apron by hemming two short and one long edge of the striped fabric. Gather up a length of 1½in (3.5cm) wide lace, baste it to the hems and stitch in place.

15 Sew running stitches along the top edge of the apron. Draw the stitches up and fit the apron tightly round the waist on top of the skirt. Cover the gathers with a long length of 1in wide (2.5cm) lace tied in a bow at the back.

16 Sew a length of 1in (2.5cm)-wide lace to go round the back of the doll and cross over the bodice. Gather small pieces of 1in (2.5cm)-wide lace and sew them to the neck and wrists.

17 Make a tiny dolly bag out of two squares of striped fabric. With wrong sides of the fabric together, machine-stitch three sides and turn right sides out.

18 Hem the open edge. Gather a length of 1in (2.5cm)-wide lace and sew it along the open edge. Fill with lavender, gather the open edge and tie a length of ribbon round the gather. Sew on a ribbon handle.

Make running stitches around the skirt top and pull threads to gather.

Make variations on the lavender lady by dressing the doll in different ways.

A fairy doll to go on the top of a Christmas tree could have yellow hair, a golden paper crown and be dressed in white silk and lace with sparkling wings made of gold cardboard. Characters from fairy tales and children's stories make excellent subjects for dolls.

23

TWO

Perfumed paper

Writing paper and ink

Sending or receiving a letter written on perfumed note paper makes the occasion a special one. If you add some scented ink, it will be a romantic gift.

Materials
Good quality writing paper
Envelopes
Sachet of pot pourri

Preparation
1 Choose a really pretty notepaper. Often this can be bought in an attractive presentation box. Remove any wrapping.

2 Place the paper in a large plastic bag with a sachet of prepared pot pourri to perfume it, for two to three weeks.

Alternatively, you could place a small sachet of pot pourri inside the box of notepaper before offering it as a present.

To scent ink, simply pour a few drops of oil of lavender or rosemary in to a bottle of ink. Stir it and replace the cap tightly.

Covering a domed box
The box in the picture was professionally covered, but it is not difficult to cover such a box yourself. All you need is a plain box, wrapping paper and wallpaper paste.

Draw a box outline like the one in the diagram to fit the box, and cut the shape out of wrapping paper.

To ensure that there are no wrinkles, dampen the wrapping paper before sticking it.

Stick bottom and sides first, pressing down all the tabs, then stick the front and back plus dome and stick all tabs.

Finally, stick the inside strip and smooth down the paper with a clean, dry cloth to remove wrinkles.

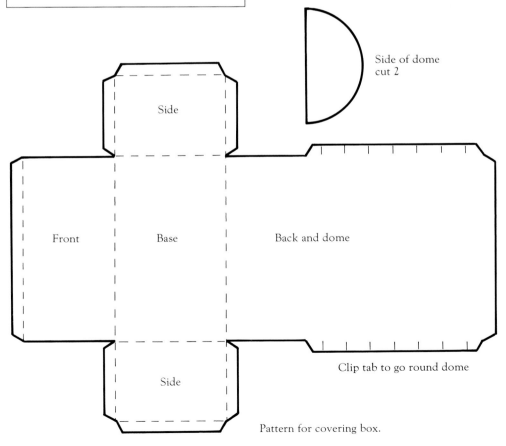

Side of dome cut 2

Side

Front

Base

Back and dome

Side

Clip tab to go round dome

Pattern for covering box.

Greetings tags

It is delightful to receive a prettily wrapped-present with a perfumed greetings tag attached to it. 3D decoupage is a simple and effective decorative technique.

Materials

Three or four identical motifs from
 giftwrap, posters or notepaper
Stiff paper or thin card for base
Hole puncher
Spray adhesive
Double sided adhesive pads
Metallic thread
Small manicure scissors with curved
 blades
Sachet of pot pourri

Preparation

1 Use the small scissors to cut out one complete design motif. Fold the stiff paper or card in half. Mount the motif on the card with spray adhesive, positioning the left hand edge of the motif against the fold.

2 Carefully cut around the motif, making sure the fold is not cut away. Open out the card and use the hole puncher to make a hole in the top left hand corner of what will be the back of the card.

Working the design

3 Cover the whole motif with sticky pads, cutting them down to size as necessary. Avoid placing them at the edge of the design where they may show. Cut out another complete motif and position this accurately over the sticky pads.

4 Look at your chosen motif and decide which areas you want to lift forward. Bear in mind that the aim is to lift the subject matter in the foreground closer, so that details which appear closest to you in the picture will be the top layer of your design. Place sticky pads over your selected areas, and cut out the relevant

details from the third motif. Stick these over the pads.

5 Continue adding sticky pads to the chosen areas and cut more details from the fourth motif. Position over the pads.

6 Cut a short length of metallic thread and slip through the hole in the card. Tie the ends together and trim.

7 Place the gift tags in a plastic bag with a sachet of pot pourri to perfume them, for two to three weeks.

Cover the motif with sticky pads.

Add more pads to the projecting areas.

Paper fan

Fans were once an essential part of the fashionable woman's wardrobe, with a language of their own. You can make an attractive modern fan out of paper.

Materials
12 × 18in (30.5 × 46cm) piece of good
quality gift wrapping paper
Spray mount adhesive
12 × 18in (30.5 × 46cm) piece of cartridge
paper
36 × ⅝in (91.5cm × 16mm) ribbon
All-purpose adhesive
Sachet of pot pourri

Preparation
1 Spray the back of the wrapping paper
with the spray mount adhesive and stick
it to the cartridge paper.

2 On the back of the cartridge paper,
mark and score lines 1in (2.5cm) apart
across the width.

Working the design
3 Fold the paper concertina-fashion
along the score lines.

4 With the paper folded, cut the top in
to a curved shape through all layers. This
will give a scalloped edge to the fan.

5 Bind the folded paper with a short
length of ribbon 4in (10cm) from the
bottom, securing the ends of the ribbon
with all-purpose adhesive. Open out the
rest of the fan.

6 Make a long-tailed bow with the
remaining ribbon and sew it to the
securing ribbon at the front of the fan.

7 Place a small sachet of pot pourri
inside the box in which you are
presenting the fan, to perfume it.

Variations on the folded paper fan
could be made by sticking thin lace
on to coloured cartridge paper, by
stencilling your own design on paper
or by making a collage out of
different pictures and sticking them
on to cartridge paper, then folding.

Front

Cutting the top of the fan.

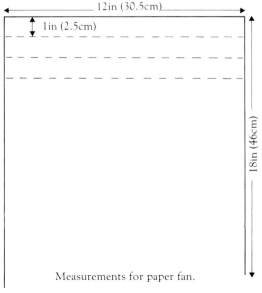

12in (30.5cm)

1in (2.5cm)

18in (46cm)

Measurements for paper fan.

31

Book markers

Book marker gifts would be suitable for children to try, with a little adult guidance. Choose coloured cards and decorate with pressed flowers or leaves.

Materials
7 × 2in (17.5 × 5cm) piece of coloured card
Pressed flowers, leaves or grasses
All-purpose adhesive
Hole puncher
⅛in (3mm)-wide Ribbon
Sachet of pot pourri

Preparation
1 Trim the corners of both the top and bottom of the card to make attractive angles.

2 Carefully position a pressed flower or leaf on the card. When satisfied with its position, fix it in place with a dab or two of glue.

3 Punch a hole in the bottom of the card and thread a ribbon through the hole.

4 Place the book marker flat in a plastic bag with a sachet of pot pourri for a few days, to perfume it.

For a more ambitious project, make a flower collage of pressed flowers and leaves to create an all-over design. You can either finish the book marker with clear varnish to protect the dried material or cover it with the clear plastic film used for covering books, which is obtainable from stationers and art shops.

Choose ribbons in shades which will tone with the card.

Another idea is to cut lengths of pretty ribbon to book marker length. Trim them top and bottom. Sew a few beads on the top to make them even more decorative.

Make a number of cards and keep them in their scented plastic bag, ready to slip in to a gift.

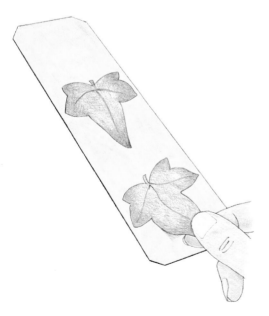

Positioning a leaf on a card.

THREE

Softly scented

Relax pillow

Beautiful bed linen makes a perfect gift and a comfortable scented pillow is particularly good for busy people. This one is scented with relaxing pot pourri.

Materials
16 × 16in (40.5 × 40cm) patterned cotton fabric
16 × 16in (40.5 × 40cm) contrasting cotton fabric for backing
Ready-made cotton pad, to fit
Sachet of pot pourri

Preparation
1 Make a small slit in the cover of the cushion pad and sew in a sachet of pot pourri. Sew up the slit.

Working the design
2 With right sides together, machine-stitch the cotton fabrics, taking a 1in (2.5cm) seam allowance.

3 Stitch round three sides of the square leaving an opening on the fourth side. Press the seams flat.

Make a small slit in the cover of the cushion pad.

4 Turn right sides out and press again. Slip in the cushion pad and sew up the opening.

If you wish, a small zip can be incorporated in to the back of the pillow so that the cover can be removed for laundering. Leave an opening large enough for the cushion pad to be inserted easily. The opening should come within 1in (2.5cm) of the two top or bottom corners at the back of the pillow.

A pretty white cotton sleep pillow of the same size could also be made, decorated with broderie anglaise lace. Scatter in some pot pourri after filling the case with a fire-retardant, polyester stuffing insert.
   A pillow like this could also serve as a ring-pillow for a wedding.

Catmint mouse

Cats love the smell of catmint and are often to be found lying in a bed of it on a warm day. Make this fun mouse filled with the herb for your special cat.

Materials
Two 8 × 5in (20 × 12.5cm) pieces of velvet or felt fabric
Dried catmint (*Napela cataria*)
10in (25.5 cm) narrow ribbon

Preparation
1 Draw a pattern from the graph pattern on squared paper and cut it out. Pin the pattern to the fabric and cut out two shapes.

2 With right sides together, pin the two shapes together, allowing a ¼in (6mm) seam allowance.

3 Machine-stitch round the mouse, leaving a small gap underneath for filling.

4 Turn right sides out.

5 Fill the mouse with dried catmint. Sew a ribbon on securely to make a long tail. Sew up the opening.

6 Embroider whiskers, eyes and nose in black cotton.

Do not use any sharp-edged buttons or beads as these could harm a cat if it chewed them, as it probably will. It is safer to use only soft materials and to embroider the features of the mouse.

Wormwood herb is excellent for ridding house pets of fleas. Mix it in to a pot pourri with dried thyme, lemon balm and sage. Fill a small pillow with the mixture and sew it in to your pets' bedding. Insects may well beat a hasty retreat!

Template for a catmint mouse.

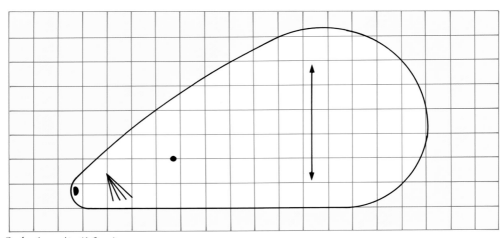

Scale: 1sq = ½in (1.2cm)

38

Coat hangers

Covered coat hangers make luxurious gifts. Here are two, a striped one for a man and a white one for a woman. Each is scented to keep clothes sweet-smelling.

Materials for striped hanger
Wooden coat hanger
Tape
62 × ½in (155cm × 3mm) satin ribbon
All-purpose Adhesive
Polyester wadding
Pot pourri
24 × 7in (61 × 18cm) striped fabric

Preparation
1 Cover the hook with tape, then bind it tightly with satin ribbon. If necessary, stick the ends of the ribbon to hold them in place.

2 Cover the hanger with two layers of wadding, sprinkling pot pourri between the layers. Fold the ends in neatly and sew or stick the wadding along the edges to secure it.

3 On the wrong side of the fabric, baste a ¼in (6mm) wide double hem along the two long edges. Machine-stitch the hems and press them.

4 Find the centre of the fabric by folding it in half lengthwise, then folding it again, in four. Carefully cut a small hole in the centre of the folds for the hook to go through, by snipping off the corner.

Working the design
5 On the right side of the fabric, machine-stitch two lengths of ribbon lengthways along each side of the centre hole, ½in (13mm) from the outer edges.

6 With right sides of the fabric together, machine-stitch the two short edges together. Turn right sides out.

7 Slip the cover over the hook on to the hanger. Pin the two hemmed edges together, then sew them with running stitch, gathering the fabric as you go to take up the fullness.

8 Gather the top edge of the fabric with running stitch in the same way. Each end of the hanger should fit closely. Attach a satin ribbon bow.

Materials for white hanger
Wooden coat hanger
Tape
12 × ⅛in (30.5cm × 3mm) satin ribbon
All-purpose adhesive
Polyester wadding
Pot pourri
24 × 7ins (61 × 18cm) white fabric
Bead trimming
16 × 3in (41cm × 7.5cm) lace

Preparation
1 Follow steps 1 to 4 for the striped hanger.

2 Omit step 5.

Working the design
3 Repeat step 6.

4 Leaving about 2in (5cm) of lace for the centre trim, gather the rest of the lace to twice the length of the bottom of the hanger.

5 Slip the cover over the hook and on to the hanger. Pin the hemmed edges together with the lace frill doubled up between them, then sew with running stitch, gathering the fabric as you go to take up the fullness.

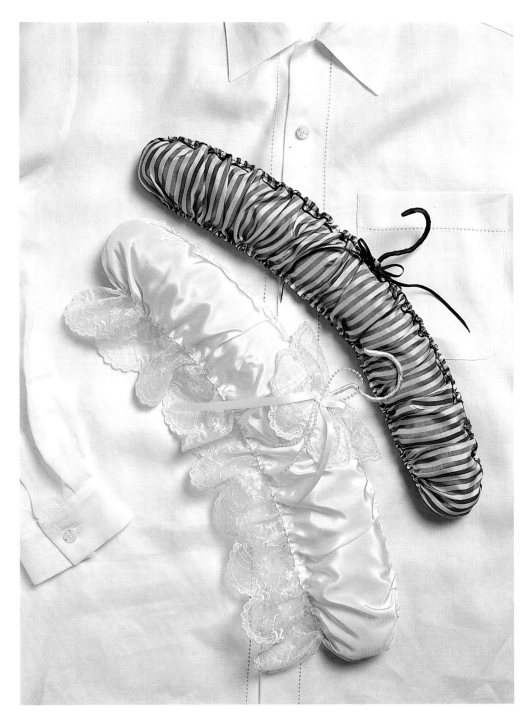

6 Gather the top of the hanger with running stitch in the same way.

7 Gather the short piece of lace so that it forms a circle. Sew it to secure the gathers, leaving a small hole, and slip it over the hook. Sew on the bead trim and a satin ribbon ribbon bow.

Heart-shaped pincushion

With the revival of interest in Victoriana, pincushions can make a romantic gift. A velvet heart with an initial picked out in pins gives this special appeal.

Materials
Two 5½ × 6 (13.5 × 16.5cm) pieces of velvet
Polyester wadding
Pot pourri
Bead trimming
Dressmakers' pins
Beads
Sequins
Narrow satin ribbon

Preparation
1 Draw a pattern from the graph pattern on squared paper and cut it out. Pin to the fabric and cut out two hearts.

Working the design
2 With right sides together and leaving a ¼in (6mm) seam allowance, stitch round two sides of the heart, leaving a section open at the top for the filling.

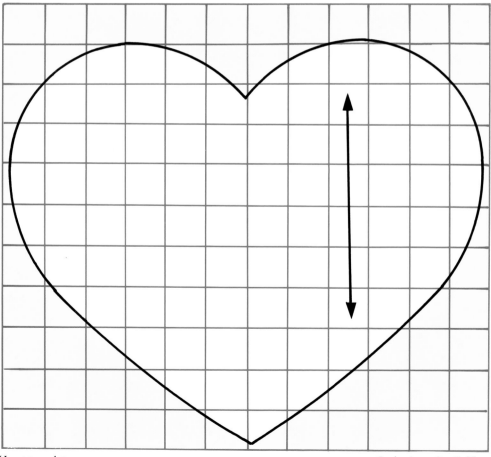

Heart template.

Scale: 1sq = ½in (1.25cm)

3 Turn right sides out and fill with polyester wadding, adding some pot pourri.

4 Sew up the open section of the heart and sew on the beaded trimming.

5 Pick out an initial in beads secured by pins. Add other sequins and beads secured by pins. Trim with a satin ribbon bow and a bead tail.

43

Nightdress and lingerie cases

Add a touch of luxury to a bedroom with these pretty lacey cases. They would make beautiful gifts, particularly if they were scented with a soft fragrance.

Materials for nightdress case
Two 30 × 13in (76.5 × 33cm) pieces of
   polyester cotton
28 × 1in (71 × 2.5cm) broderie anglaise
   eyelet ribbon
2yd × 3in (2m × 8cm) broderie anglaise
   frilling
Pot pourri
Polyester wadding
3yd × ⅛in (3m × 3mm) satin ribbon
18 × ½in (46 × 13mm) satin ribbon

Preparation
1 Machine-stitch two rows of broderie
anglaise eyelet ribbon, 3in (8cm) and 6in
(15.5cm) from the top of the narrow edge
of one piece of polyester cotton.
Machine-stitch two tucks above and two
tucks below the eyelet ribbons.

2 Baste the broderie anglaise frill to the
right side of the top edge and one third
of the way down two long sides of the
same piece of fabric with the frill facing
the centre of the fabric.

Working the design
3 With right sides together, place the
second piece of fabric on top of the frill,
so that it is sandwiched between the two
pieces of polyester cotton.

4 Sprinkle pot pourri on the top piece of
polyester cotton and lay a piece of
polyester wadding the same size on top.

5 Leaving a ¼in (6mm) seam allowance,
tack and then machine-stitch all round
the edges, leaving a small gap at the
bottom for turning.

6 Turn right sides out. Sew up gap.

7 Turn up the bottom half of the case to
form an envelope. Sew in place. Press
flat. Thread double ribbon through the
eyelets. Finish both ends with bows.

Materials for lingerie case
96 × 3½in (240 × 9cm) lace
Two 10 × 30in (25 × 76cm) pieces of
   polyester satin
Pot pourri
Polyester wadding

Preparation
1 Gather half the lace to make a frill and
baste it to the right side of the top edge
and down one third of two long sides of
one of the pieces of satin, with the frill
facing the centre of the fabric.

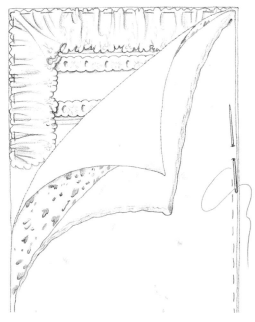

Working the design

2 Follow steps 5 to 8 for the nightdress case.

3 Gather the remaining half of the lace to make another frill and sew it in a V shape to the front of the case. Decorate with a ribbon rose on a ribbon bow.

Herb bags

Crisp gingham bags filled with a sweet-smelling herb mixture of pot pourri will brighten up a kitchen and would make a very welcome house-warming gift.

Materials
Several 4½in (11.5cm) diameter circles of gingham fabric
Equal number 3½in (9cm) circles of muslin
Pinking shears
Pot pourri
Ribbon

Preparation
1 Trim the edges of the gingham fabric circles with pinking shears.

2 Sew a line of running stitches around the edge of each circle. Do not make fast the ends of the thread.

Working the design
3 Put a small scoop of the pot pourri in the centre of the muslin circles. Draw up the edges to form a small bag and secure it by sewing.

4 Place the muslin bags in the gingham circles and draw up the edges to make a bag. Secure the opening with ribbon.

Several gingham bags in a pretty glass storage jar will make an acceptable gift. Here is a recipe for herb mix pot pourri:
1 cup of crushed peppermint leaves
1 cup of cologne mint leaves
1 cup of shredded bay leaves
1 cup of sage and rosemary leaves
1 teaspoon of powdered clove
1 teaspoon of mixed spice

Filling the inner muslin bag.

FOUR

Wedding gifts

Horseshoe

Brides love to receive a good luck token and, as a real horseshoe would look somewhat out of place, a pretty fabric one would make an attractive substitute.

Materials
Two 6 × 6½in (15 × 16cm) pieces of silk
  fabric
40 × 1½in (101.5 × 4cm) lace
Polyester wadding
Pot pourri
20 × 1in (51 × 2.5cm) satin ribbon
30 × ⅛in (76cm × 3mm) blue satin ribbon
30 × ⅛in (76cm × 3mm) white satin ribbon
Bead trimming; pearl beads

Preparation
1 Draw a pattern from the graph pattern on squared paper and cut it out. Pin to the silk fabric and cut out two shapes.

2 Leaving about 6in (15cm) of lace for the lace motif, pleat and baste the lace to the right side of the outside edge of one of the horseshoe shapes.

Working the design
3 With right sides together baste the two horseshoe pieces together with the lace sandwiched between them. Taking a ¼in (6mm) seam allowance, machine-stitch all the way round, leaving an opening.

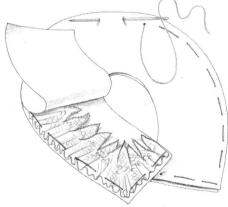

Frill attached to right side of one shape.

4 Turn right sides out. Stuff firmly with wadding, adding pot pourri as you fill. Sew up the opening and sew the ribbon loop to the top of the horseshoe.

5 To decorate, make satin roses by tightly coiling lengths of blue ribbon, or if you prefer, make a neat bow. Sew on loops of blue and white satin ribbon and bead trim to hang from the roses or bow.

6 Gather the rest of the lace to make a small lace motif and sew it to the front of the horseshoe near the bottom. Add a cluster of pearl beads to the motif.

Graph pattern for horseshoe

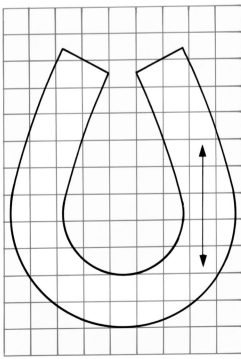

Scale: 1 sq = ½in (1.2cm)

Shoe roses

Decorate a pair of plain wedding shoes with these silk roses. They need a little practice at first but the same method is used for ribbon or fabric.

Materials
30 × 3in (76 × 7.5cm) silk fabric
Bought shoe clips
Sachet of pot pourri

Preparation
1 Fold the fabric in half lengthways. Press.

2 Taper the fabric at one end of the strip to form an elongated wedge shape. Do not cut the folded edge.

Working the design
3 On a flat surface and starting from the narrow end of the strip with the folded edge at the top, coil and pleat the fabric in to a loose rose shape.

4 Aim to create a flat, squashy shape with a tightly-rolled centre surrounded by three layers of 'petals'. Experiment with several roses, then secure with small stitches as you go.

5 Sew the clip to the back of the rose. Place the shoe clips in a bag with a sachet of pot pourri for two to three weeks to perfume them.

For added decoration, sew a small pearl or crystal bead in the centre of the rose.
  Roses look pretty in patterned fabric, but whatever fabric is used, it must be lightweight. A matt fabric is easier to roll and pleat than a shiny one.
  The roses can be sewn directly on to fabric shoes.

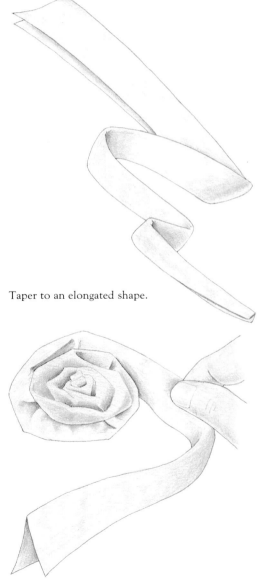

Taper to an elongated shape.

Coil from the narrow end with folded edge on the top.

Garter

A scented garter is another lovely gift for a bride. This one is quite easy to make but the lace and satin make it look elaborate and glamorous.

Materials
30 × ½in (76cm × 13mm) satin ribbon
30 × 3in (76 × 7.5cm) lace
15½ × ¼in (39.5 × 6mm) elastic
1yd × ⅛in (1m × 3mm) satin ribbon for
  roses and bows
Bead trim
Sachet of pot pourri

Preparation
1 Stitch the ½in (13mm)-wide ribbon on to a length of lace ½in (13mm) down from the top. Stitch both edges of the ribbon.

Working the design
2 Thread the elastic through the ribbon, gathering up the lace as you go. Secure the ends of the elastic and the ribbon.

3 Sew the ends of the elastic, ribbon and lace together to form a garter.

4 Press with a cool iron.

5 Trim with satin roses, bows and bead trim.

6 Place in a bag with a sachet of pot pourri to perfume it.

Trim with satin roses, bows and bead trim.

Stitching ribbon to a length of lace.

> You could use narrow white or blue velvet ribbon instead of satin ribbon and trim the garter with tiny silk flowers.

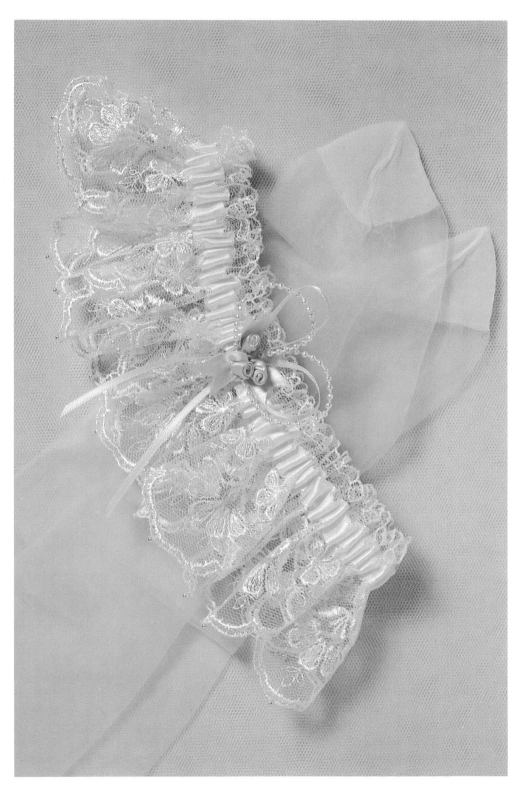

Bridal bag

This pretty drawstring bag could be a useful accessory for a bride to carry on her wedding day. Made of silk and lace, the fabric could match her gown.

Materials
15 × 5½in (38 × 14cm) lace
15 × 5½in (38 × 14cm) silk fabric
15 × ½in (38cm × 13mm) satin ribbon
5in (12.5cm)-diameter circle of silk fabric
    for the base
Sachet of pot pourri
36 × ¼in (91.5cm × 6mm) satin ribbon for
    drawstrings

Preparation
1 Lay the lace on the right side of the
silk fabric. Make a French seam down
the narrow side of the fabric to form an
open-ended tube. (This will hide the raw
edges.)

Working the design
2 Turn over one raw edge of the tube to
make a seam on the right side of the
fabric. Press.

3 Cut the ½in (13mm) satin ribbon in half
to make two pieces 7½in (19cm) long.

4 Turn under the four narrow ends of
the ribbons and machine-stitch the two
lengths of ribbon on to the silk and lace
tube so that they cover the raw edge of
the seam on the right side. This will make
a neat casing for the drawstring.

5 With right sides together, baste and
then machine-stitch the circle of fabric to
the bottom of the tube, forming a bag.
Oversew or bind the seam to neaten it.

6 Sew a small sachet of pot pourri inside
the bag.

Threading the ribbon through the casing.

7 Turn right sides out and thread two
lengths of narrow ribbon through the
ribbon casing. Sew the ends of the
ribbons to make two continuous loops
and pull them on either side of the bag to
make ribbon drawstrings of even length.

This drawstring bag could be made
out of any fabric, and it could be any
size.
   It would make an excellent
cosmetic bag or a useful sewing hold-
all to take away on holiday filled with
needles, thread, thimble and a small
pair of scissors, all of which are
handy in an emergency.

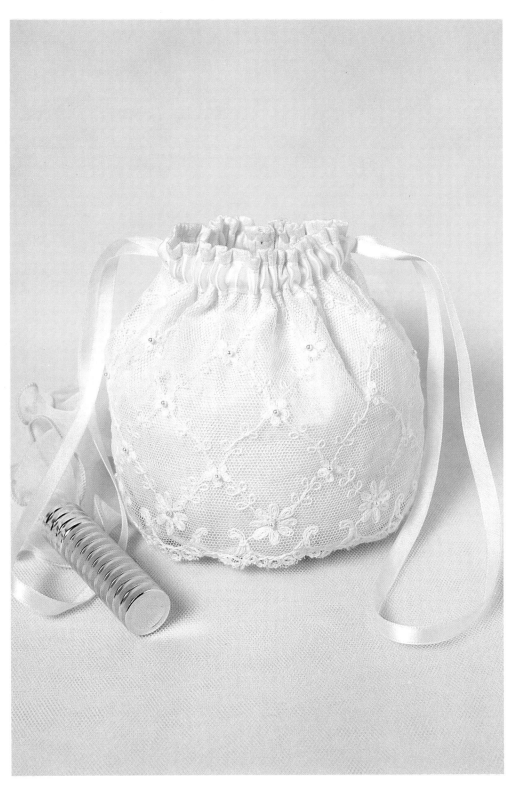

Dried flowers

Flowers in eggshells

A pretty basket containing eggshells filled with tiny posies of dried flowers will make a delightful and unusual gift to offer on an Easter morning.

Materials
Bought rustic basket
Eggshells
Coloured tissue paper
Dried hydrangea
Dried yellow yarrow
Dried pink and red statice
Grasses
Carnation oil
22 gauge florist's wire

Preparation
1 Wash and dry the egg shells. Cut them in half and trim the edges.

2 Line the basket with tissue paper.

3 Place the eggshells in the basket, arranging them so that the tissue paper cushions each shell.

Tuck short pieces of statice in the handle of the basket.

Wire stems to make tiny posies to fit in eggshells.

Working the design
4 Snip short the stems of some of the flowers and wire them together to make tiny posies to fit in to the eggshells. Mix the colours to get a nice bright, natural effect.

5 Tuck short pieces of statice in to the handle of the basket and round the edges to add some extra colour.

6 Perfume the flowers with a few drops of carnation oil.

Another way of adding perfume to this arrangement of flowers in eggshells would be to tuck a sachet of pot pourri underneath the tissue paper lining.
  Either of the 'Rose dream' or 'Lavender time' pot pourri recipes would provide a suitable fragrance.

60

Flower head mosaic

A dried flower mosaic set in a decorative box makes this an unusual table centre. It is also delicately perfumed, and would make a delightful housewarming gift.

Materials
Hexagonal gift box
Florist's dry foam
Dried teazels
Dried rosemary, dyed blue
Dried gold yarrow
Dried love-in-a-mist
Dried pink and cream canary grass
Dried poppy heads
Dried white statice
Citronella oil

Preparation
1 Cut a hexagonal piece of florist's dry foam to fit the gift box.

Working the design
2 Cut a teazel so that the stem is 2in (5cm) long and insert it in to the centre of the foam.

3 Cut the rosemary so that it is 2in (5cm) long and insert it at the edge of the foam to make a border of rosemary inside the outer edge of the box. Pack the flowers closely together.

4 Following the diagram and starting at the edge next to the rosemary, insert yarrow, love-in-a-mist, canary grass and poppy heads, filling any spaces with white statice.

5 Aim to achieve an even, closely packed design with no gaps. You will soon see the mosaic pattern emerging.

6 Add a few drops of citronella oil to the teazel to perfume it.

Plan of flower mosaic.
R – Rosemary
L – Love-in-a-mist
CG – Canary grass
Y – Yarrow
P – Poppy heads
S – White statice

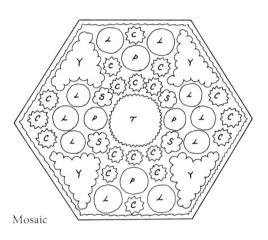

Mosaic

There are so many varieties of container to be found in the shops. Confectioners are particularly imaginative in their use of gift boxes, especially at Christmas time.
  Save any pretty boxes you may be given. They always come in useful and it would be a charming idea to return one to the donor, filled with dried flowers!

Dried flower posy

Posies of aromatic flowers and herbs were popular in the past. This posy of long lasting, perfumed dried flowers, could be used on more than one occasion.

Materials
Dried cream helichrysum
Dried blue and yellow statice
Dried pink canary grass
Dried mauve sea lavender
22 gauge florist's wire
White stem tape
Silver wire
Cream and pink satin ribbon
Bought lace posy holder
Spotted net
Bergamot oil

Preparation
1 Wire each of the flowers on to florist's wire and cover the wires with stem tape.

Bind the stems with tape.

Working the design
2 Surround a piece of blue statice with five cream helichrysum flowers. Bind the stems together with silver wire.

3 Bind in the pink canary grass and yellow statice.

4 Continue placing and binding in the remainder of the flowers, aiming for a closely packed design. Finish with an outside circle of sea lavender and some cream ribbon bows.

5 Bind the stems with tape. Wind pink ribbon round the binding to cover it and slip the completed posy in the lace posy holder.

6 Make some ribbon bows and twist them on to wire so that they can nestle among the flowers in the holder. Make a spotted net bow to go round the bound stems.

Ribbon folded in to two loops.

Twist wire round to secure.

7 Add a few drops of bergamot oil to the centre flowers.

Herb garland

The kitchen is often overlooked when it comes to making gifts but a garland of dried herbs on a gnarled twig would give a kitchen a fresh country look.

Materials
Bought medium-sized twig wreath
Dried grasses
Dried sage
Dried rosemary
Dried wheat heads
Dried bay leaves
22 gauge florist's wire
1yd (1m) Ribbon
Green stem binding

Preparation
1 Trim the dried material to make short, workable pieces.

2 Wire pieces of grass, sage and rosemary in to small bunches.

3 Wire wheat heads and bay leaves separately in twos and threes.

4 Wire the ribbon in small bows.

5 Bind all the wires with stem binding.

Working the design
6 Aiming for a fairly loose, rustic style, insert the wired bunches of grass, sage, rosemary and wheat heads in the garland. Make all the herbs and grasses flow in the same direction.

7 Secure the herbs to the garland with wire and stem binding.

8 Continue round the garland leaving roughly 2ins (5cm) between each group of herbs.

9 Fill in with the wired bay leaves and tuck in wired ribbon bows to finish.

Herbs and grasses should 'flow' in the same direction.

Garlands are particularly welcome at Christmas time, when their bright colours bring a note of gaiety to the festivities.

When making a Christmas wreath, it would be quite easy to tuck some sweet-smelling herbs among the holly and the ivy and let them add their fragrance to the house.

Pine cone basket

Pine cones arranged in an old fashioned basket are always a firm seasonal favourite. This particular basket has had a bow added to it for extra interest.

Materials
Large basket
Pine cones
Helichrysum
Green fabric for basket lining
46 × 10in (117 × 25.5cm) piece of muslin
24 × 1½in (61 × 4cm) piece of muslin
Latex adhesive
20 gauge florists' wire
Pine oil

Preparation
1 Select, dry and clean pine cones and leave them to open their seeds in a warm, dry room.

2 Measure a piece of green fabric to fit inside the basket. Apply glue to the edges and fold over a small hem all round to neaten.

3 Line the basket with the prepared fabric.

Working the design
4 Arrange cones neatly in the basket on the green fabric.

5 Wire some small cones to the basket handle.

6 Arrange some helichrysum heads among the cones.

7 Make a muslin bow by folding the large piece of muslin in three lengthways and tie it in a floppy bow round the handle.

8 Tie the narrow strip of muslin to the opposite side of the handle.

9 Add a few drops of pine oil to the cones.

If you stand the basket near the fire, the pine perfume will fill the room with lovely fragrance.

Pomander

Pomanders were once carried by wealthy people to ward off sickness. Though they are no longer valued as a prophylactic, they make an aromatic gift for a friend.

Materials
Tape
An orange
Pins
Knitting needle
Whole cloves with buds intact
Orris root powder
Ground cinnamon
Tissue paper
Ribbon

Preparation
1 Wind tape round the orange so that it is divided into four quarters. Pin the tape to the top and bottom of the orange and at the sides.

Working the design
2 Using the knitting needle and working one quarter at a time, pierce the skin of the fruit and insert the cloves in to the holes.

3 Follow the lines of the tape and insert cloves in lines until the skin is covered.

4 Mix orris root with the cinnamon. Roll the orange in the powder mixture and shake off the excess. (The powders will preserve the orange and give it a spicey fragrance.)

5 Wrap the orange in tissue paper and place it in a brown paper bag for three to five weeks in a warm, dry place. Allow the fruit to dry completely.

6 Remove the tape and replace it with ribbon. Make a hanging loop at the top by folding a length of ribbon and pinning it in place. As the fruit dries it will shrink. The spicey fragrance will last a long time.

> You can also make a pomander out of a lemon. Wind the tape round the centre of the lemon only, then follow the instructions for the orange pomander.
> Pomanders can be hung in clothes cupboards, where they will retain their pleasant smell for some time.

Use a knitting needle to pierce the fruit skin.

SIX

Better Techniques

❦

Read this chapter before starting a project. Amongst other things, it will give you useful information on making pot pourri and drying and wiring flowers.

POT POURRI

Pot pourri captures the fragrance of dried flowers, herbs, aromatic seeds and foliage. Once you have mastered a few basic techniques, it is easy to create your own different pot pourri mixtures.

Drying flowers

Nearly any flower, herb, grass, seed or foliage is suitable for use in pot pourri.

Choose healthy pieces and try to gather them on a dry day. Discard bruised or damaged materials.

Spread the flower heads on sheets of newspaper and leave them in a warm, airy place to dry completely.

Whole rosebuds can be gathered and left to dry separately or you can hang them upside down in bunches of five roses with leaves intact in a warm airy place to dry. Herbs and lavender can be cut and hung upside down from the ceiling in small bunches to dry.

Check after about a week to see if the material is dry enough to use. It should feel papery and firm, not limp or damp.

Dried rose petals are an important ingredient in many pot pourri recipes. They keep their colour well.

Store prepared material in an airtight container such as a used ice cream carton with a lid. Keep flower groups separate, roses in one, lavender in another and so on. They will keep well like this in a cool place until you are ready to use them.

The dried material will have a natural fragrance but this will soon fade if you do not use a fixative. Orris root is one of the best, but you can also use spices from the store cupboard such as cinnamon, mixed spice, cloves, nutmeg, sea salt, lemon and orange peel.

Essential oils

These are another vital fixative which will add depth and intensity of fragrance to pot pourri mixtures.

Essential oils are made by distilling different kinds of plant material.

All essential oils must be used very carefully. They should not be taken internally, be used directly on the skin or used as aromatherapy oils.

They are purely an added ingredient for pot pourri and other scented projects.

Roses, herbs and lavender hung to dry.

Keep them away from varnished wood and other fine surfaces, as drops of oil will stain.

Keep oils away from naked flame and avoid contact with hands, as the oil has a very strong perfume.

Never store the oils in plastic bottles but keep them in the glass bottles in which they were purchased.

Always use a dropper when adding oil. Store oil in a cool place with the cap tightly fixed, out of sight and reach of children and animals.

Use it sparingly, one drop at a time, as too much will upset the delicate balance of pot pourri fragrance.

How to make pot pourri

Part of the fun of making pot pourri is in inventing your own mixtures, adding different herbs or flowers or mixing oils and spices to produce an individual fragrance.

Look for texture and colour as well as fragrance. Try to save a few whole flowers to scatter on top of pot pourri when you have made it.

Combine all the ingredients in a large wooden or glass bowl. Then add the fixatives, orris root powder, herbs, spices, salt, to 'hold' the perfume and finally add the drops of essential oil. Stir the mixture to spread the contents.

Store pot pourri in an airtight container for four to six weeks. This length of time will ensure that it has matured and will hold its perfume. If the mint leaves are too large, tear them in smaller pieces.

POT POURRI RECIPES
Lavender time

A traditional recipe suitable for perfuming linen.
4 cups of lavender flowers
2 cups of lemon mint leaves
1 cup of dried thyme
½ cup of coarse salt
1 tablespoon of powdered cloves
1 tablespoon of dried lemon peel
2 or 3 drops of lavender oil

Country breeze

A pretty pot pourri you can use to fill a sachet for a sleep pillow.
3 cups of red rose petals
2 cups of pink clover flowers
2 cups of apple mint leaves
1 cup of marjoram and sage leaves, mixed
1 cup of rose geranium leaves
1 cup of pink statice flowers
1 tablespoon of grated lemon peel
2 tablespoons of orris root powder
2 or 3 drops of rose geranium oil

Wild flower pot pourri

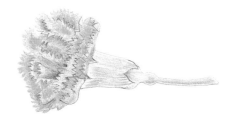

This evocative mixture works well in wedding gift projects.
3 cups of pink rose petals
3 cups of clove variety carnation petals
2 cups of camomile flowers
1 cup of lavender flowers
1 cup of lemon verbena leaves
2 teaspoons of orris root powder
1 teaspoon of powdered cloves
2 or 3 drops of carnation oil

Rose dream

An original perfume. Use it for scenting
   drawer liners and writing paper.
5 cups of strong scented rose petals
4 bay leaves finely chopped
2 vanilla pods finely chopped
1 tablespoon of ground nutmeg
1 tablespoon of cinnamon powder
1 tablespoon of orris root powder

Pine walk

This invigorating pine fragrance can be
   used to perfume a coat hanger or a
   pillow.
3 cups of well-dried pine shavings
2 cups of shredded bay leaves
2 cups of shredded lemon balm leaves
1 cup of golden rod flowers
1 cup of peppermint leaves
2 teaspoons of mixed spice
2 teaspoons of orris root powder
2 or 3 drops of pine oil

Flowers suitable for pot pourri

Chamomile, geranium, golden rod,
heather, lavender, lemon balm, marigold,
pansy, rose, salvia, strawflower, tansy,
yarrow.

Herbs to discourage insects

Basil, bay, elder, meadowsweet, mint,
pennyroyal, rosemary, rue,
southernwood, wormwood.

DEALING WITH DRIED FLOWERS
Wires and wiring

Wires can be purchased from florist's
shops, usually in small bundles.

For the projects in this book, three
sorts of wire have been used. They are
standard wire gauge nos. 22 and 20 (12in,
30cm long) and fine silver wire.

Attaching wires to flowers and other
material makes it easier to arrange them.
Take a flower in one hand and carefully
bind the wire three times round the stem.

Binding with stem tape

Wired flower stems need to be covered
with stem tape (or gutta percha), which is
available in various shades from florist's
shops.

Hold the wired flower in one hand
and, starting at the top of the wire, twist
and firmly pull the stem tape round it
until the wire is covered.

Wiring fir cones

Take one end of a 12in (30cm) no. 20
wire. Push it between the lowest seeds of
the fir cone, leaving about 1½in (4cm) of
wire protruding. Tightly wind the long
end of the wire in and out of the seeds
until both ends of the wire meet. Twist
the two wire ends together to secure
them. Trim them, cover them with stem
tape and bend them under the base of the
cone.

Silk flowers

Silk flowers are widely obtainable and
useful for scented projects. They are also
easy to handle and individual pieces can
be snipped off the main stem with sharp
scissors. They can then be wired or sewn
in to an arrangement. They can be gently
wiped with a damp cloth to remove dust,
or carefully handwashed in luke warm
water and left to dry away from heat
sources.

It is worth while taking time to select
natural-looking material.

Pressing flowers

Many different types of flowers, herbs
and foliage are suitable for pressing but

avoid fleshy specimens, as they do not press well.

You can use a flower press or, easier still, place items between sheets of blotting paper and press in a heavy book.

Gather material on a dry day, choosing only perfect pieces. Spread them on sheets of blotting paper so that they do not touch each other.

Place them under a pile of heavy books and leave them for about four to six weeks to dry. Some materials such as petals, leaves and grasses, dry faster than others, so check regularly. The material will change to muted shades when dry.

Experiment with different kinds of flowers and grasses until you have built up a collection ready for use.

Once pressed, remove the blotting paper with tweezers and store flat between clean sheets of paper.

Some flowers suitable for pressing are buttercup, daisy, freesia, pansy, primula, rose, violet, foliage and grasses.

Florist's foam

Two kinds of foam are used in floral arrangements, brown, which is dry and used for dried flower arrangements, (available in blocks, balls, cones and cylinders) and green, sold in blocks and used for wet arrangements. This must be soaked in water before use.

MAKING BOWS
Ribbon bows for wiring

To make ribbon bows as a final touch to a gift, form a length of ribbon in a figure of eight, holding the centre between thumb and forefinger. With the same length of ribbon, make another figure of eight. Hold the bows together at the centre and bind them together with lightweight wire, leaving two wire 'legs'.

If you find this is too difficult, use several single loops on top of each other.

Sewn ribbon bows

Cut a length of ribbon in two, with one piece slightly shorter than the other. Fold the ends of the longer piece in to the

middle, overlapping slightly. Sew a gathering thread across the centre and tie tightly. Fold the shorter piece in half round the waist of the bow. Sew in place at the back to form the knot. Arrange the ends neatly and trim.

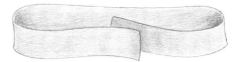

Fold the ends to the middle.

Sew across the centre.

Gather up tightly and tie off.

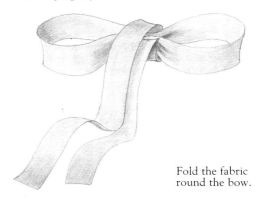

Fold the fabric round the bow.

Ribbons.

Fabric bows

Use a strip of fabric twice as wide as the ribbon required plus ½in (13mm). Fold the strip in half lengthways with right sides facing and stitch along the length, taking a ¼in (6mm) seam, leaving the ends open. Press the seam open. Turn right side out and press the strip so that the seam is at the back. Form the bow in the same way as for sewn ribbon bows and finish by tucking in the raw edges. Oversew the ends.

Decorative trimmings

Ribbons and braids come in most widths and colours. As well as plain ribbons in satin, grosgrain, velvet or taffeta there are printed ribbons and many decoratively-edged ribbons.

Cutting a stencil.

Sew narrow ribbons and braids with one line of central stitching. Machine-stitch wider ribbons down both edges, always stitching in the same direction to prevent puckering.

Lace also comes in a variety of patterns and widths. Choose cotton lace if the item is to be ironed.

Pretty broderie anglaise is available flat with slots for ribbon insertion, and pre-gathered.

Beaded trimming is also obtainable.

STENCILLING

You can create your own stencil designs freehand or copy or trace an illustration from a book or picture. When you have chosen a design, draw it on to tracing paper, then transfer it to card or a piece of acetate.

To cut the stencil you will need either very sharp, short pointed scissors or a craft knife.

Always cut stencils on a firm, protected surface and be extra careful when handling sharp tools, keeping fingers well out of the way.

Mark the card or acetate sheet with a fine waterproof felt-tipped pen.

If you plan to use more than one colour, you will need separate stencils for each colour.

Acrylic paints are suitable for most projects, fabric paints are suitable for fabrics and you can make a quick stencil on paper with felt-tipped pens.

Short, stubby brushes especially for stencilling can be purchased from art shops but almost any brush can be used on small projects.

Clear and spray varnish can be used to protect a design.

Painting a stencil.

SEWING TECHNIQUES
Scissors
For basic sewing you need two pairs of scissors, a large pair for cutting out and a small, sharply-pointed pair for snipping threads and so on.

All scissors must be sharp but especially when cutting out, so keep them so.

Most types can be sharpened on a kitchen knife sharpener.

Never use dressmaking scissors for cutting out heavy paper or card as this will damage the cutting edge and the scissors will be useless for cutting fabric.

Avoid cutting across pins when cutting out as this, too, can damage the blades.

Measuring
A good tape measure is essential. It must be made from non-stretch material and have metal ends. The tape will be more useful if imperial measurements are marked on one side with metric measurements on the reverse. However, when working the projects in this book, do not try to combine the two.

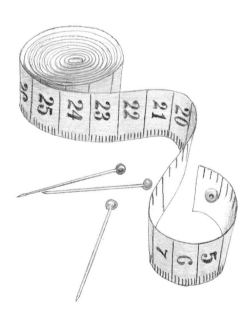

A good tape measure and sharp pins are essential.

Pins
For most sewing, use fine, standard length pins, making sure that they are sharp, as blunt pins can snag the fabric. Discard those if you find them. Decorative pins with pearl tops can be used to decorate pincushions, or to secure a ribbon bow.

Needles
Needles are grouped according to their use. For general sewing, use 'sharps', which are available in sizes 3–10. The higher the number, the finer the needle. If you prefer a shorter needle, use a 'between'.

When hand sewing, wear a thimble on the middle finger of the sewing hand. This will help push the needle through tough fabrics and prevent your finger from becoming sore.

If you find threading a needle difficult, use a needle-threader. For general embroidery, a mixed packet of crewel needles is sufficient.

Sewing threads
One of the most important materials in any sewing is the thread. Always match the type of thread to the fabric, i.e. silk with silk and cotton with cotton. For mixed-fibre fabrics, choose an all-purpose thread.

Match the thread to the colour of the fabric. The various brands of thread available all have good colour ranges from which to choose and, as a general rule, pick thread that is one shade darker than the fabric you are using.

Use soft, loosely-twisted basting thread.

Wadding
Wadding is a layer of fabric that is sandwiched between two other fabrics to pad it. It is also a filling that is used to stuff things.

Washable polyester wadding comes in different weights from light to extra heavyweight (for upholstery). Use lightweight wadding to give fabric extra body and also for stuffing.

SEWING STITCHES
Basting

This is a temporary stitch used to hold two layers of fabric together while the permanent stitching is worked.

Fasten the thread either with a knot or with a double back stitch on the spot. Take $\frac{1}{2}$in (13mm)-long stitches through both fabrics. After the main stitching, snip off the knot (or unpick the back stitches) and pull out the basting.

Running stitch

Running stitch and gathering.

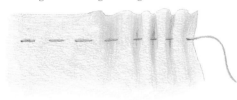

A stitch used for gathering or when stitching fine seams by hand. Work from right to left. Begin with two or three back stitches on the spot. Pass the needle in and out of the fabric, making small, evenly-spaced stitches about $\frac{1}{8}$in (3mm) long.

Back stitch

A strong, hardwearing stitch which looks like machine stitching when properly worked. It is an ideal stitch to use when sewing seams by hand.

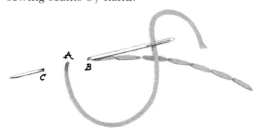

Back stitch.

Work from right to left. Begin with two or three stitches on the spot then work a running stitch and a space, take the needle back over the space, bringing it out the same distance away.

Oversewing

This stitch is useful for joining the edges of fabric together and can also be used to neaten seam edges to prevent them from fraying.

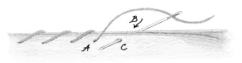

Oversewing.

Working from left to right, bring the needle through at A and insert the needle from the back of the work at B, bringing it through to the front at C ready to start the next stitch. Keep stitches small and evenly spaced.

French seam

This is a seam stitched twice, once from the right side of the fabric and once from the wrong side.

French seam.

With wrong sides of fabric together, stitch a $\frac{1}{2}$in (13mm) seam from the edge. Trim the seam allowance to $\frac{1}{8}$in (3mm). Press the seam open. Fold right sides together with the stitched line on the fold. Press again. Stitch a seam $\frac{1}{8}$in (3mm) from the fold.

PATTERN MAKING MATERIALS

The patterns in this book are given in two forms, direct trace-offs and as diagrams. You may sometimes meet another form of pattern – the graph pattern.

Some equipment will be required to prepare patterns for doll making.

Direct trace-off patterns

To use these, you will need sheets of tracing paper or kitchen greaseproof paper. The tracing paper is laid over the book page and taped down at the edges with small pieces of Sellotape or Scotchtape. Trace the image with a sharply-pointed HB pencil.

Very simple shapes may be drawn directly on to the wrong side of smooth fabrics, in soft pencil or dressmaker's chalk pencil. If fabrics are transparent, full-sized patterns can be direct-traced from the page, using a finely sharpened HB pencil, or a coloured embroidery pencil. Another useful marking device is a pen which has air-soluble ink in it. After tracing a pattern the line remains on the fabric for a short time before it disappears.

Diagram patterns

Copy these on to squared graph paper, using a ruler and a sharp HB pencil.

The lines on the paper will help you to keep corners square and accurate. You may find a flexible plastic ruler an aid when drawing curves. The ruler can be easily bent into a curve and then you simply pencil along its edge. The pattern shapes can either be cut directly from the graph paper or, if you wish to keep the pattern for repeated use, trace it on to tracing paper.

Graph patterns

These patterns are given reduced in size on a squared grid. A scale is given and, to produce a full-sized pattern, you need squared dressmaker's paper marked with squares of the same scale. This paper is sold in large sheets, several to a packet, and can be obtained from dressmaking notions counters in shops and department stores.

To reproduce a graph pattern you copy the lines on your pattern paper, square for square. Graph patterns are not given for any of the projects in this book.

Transferring patterns

Patterns are transferred to the fabric with dressmaker's carbon paper. This is sold in sheets in packets of three or four colours, red, blue, yellow and white. A sheet is slipped between the pattern and fabric, and then the lines traced over with a tracing tool or a sharply-pointed HB pencil.

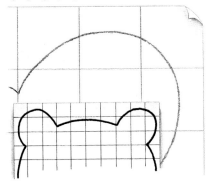

Enlarging a graph pattern.

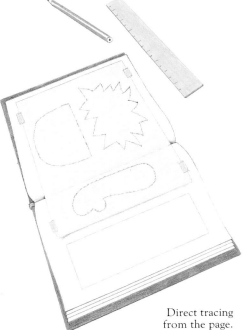

Direct tracing from the page.

Acknowledgements

The author would like to thank Offray
ribbons for their help and also Sarah
Waeschle of 'The Silkworm', Millstream
Close, Wimborne, Dorset, BH21 1DW;
Susan Saron of 'Nosegay', Walford Mill,
Wimborne, Dorset, and Kerrie Dudley,
who made the fan
The publishers would like to thank
Margaret Lee for supplying the shoes on
page 48 In photography. For further
information on these and other bridal
shoes, telephone 0702 616180.